Compound Christmas Ornaments
for the Scroll Saw

By Diana Thompson

Fox Chapel Publishing Co. Inc.

1970 Broad Street • East Petersburg, PA 17520 • www.foxchapelpublishing.com

Acknowledgments

Thank you Father. When prayers go up, blessings come down!
Thanks to John Nelson, "great instigator" and legendary designer, for the challenge to design
a 3-D piece with lots of pieces. The poinsettia arrangement on page 56 is the result.
Thanks to my editor, Ayleen Stellhorn, who requested something I'd never thought I could
do justice to — the nativity scene on page 63.

Compound Christmas Ornaments for the Scroll Saw is a brand new work, first published in 2003 by Fox Chapel
Publishing Company, Inc. The patterns contained herein are copyrighted by the author. Artists purchasing this
book have permission to make up to 200 cutouts of each individual pattern. Persons or companies
wishing to make more than 200 cutouts must notify the author in writing for permission. The patterns
themselves, however, are not to be duplicated for resale or distribution under any circumstances.

Publisher	Alan Giagnocavo
Book Editor	Ayleen Stellhorn
Desktop Specialist	Alan Davis
Cover Design	Tim Mize
Interior Gallery Photos	Keren Holl

ISBN # 1–56523–181–3
Library of Congress Preassigned Card Number: 2002102710

To order your copy of this book,
please send check or money order
for the cover price plus $3.00 shipping to:
Fox Books
1970 Broad Street
East Petersburg, PA 17520

Or visit us on the web at
www.foxchapelpublishing.com

Manufactured in Korea
10 9 8 7 6 5 4 3 2 1

Because scrolling wood and other materials inherently includes the risk of injury and damage, this book
cannot guarantee that creating the projects in this book is safe for everyone. For this reason, this book is
sold without warranties or guarantees of any kind, express or implied, and the publisher and author dis-
claim any liability for any injuries, losses or damages caused in any way by the content of this book or
the reader's use of the tools needed to complete the projects presented here. The publisher and author
urge all scrollers to thoroughly review each project and to understand the use of all tools
involved before beginning any project.

Table of Contents

Introduction

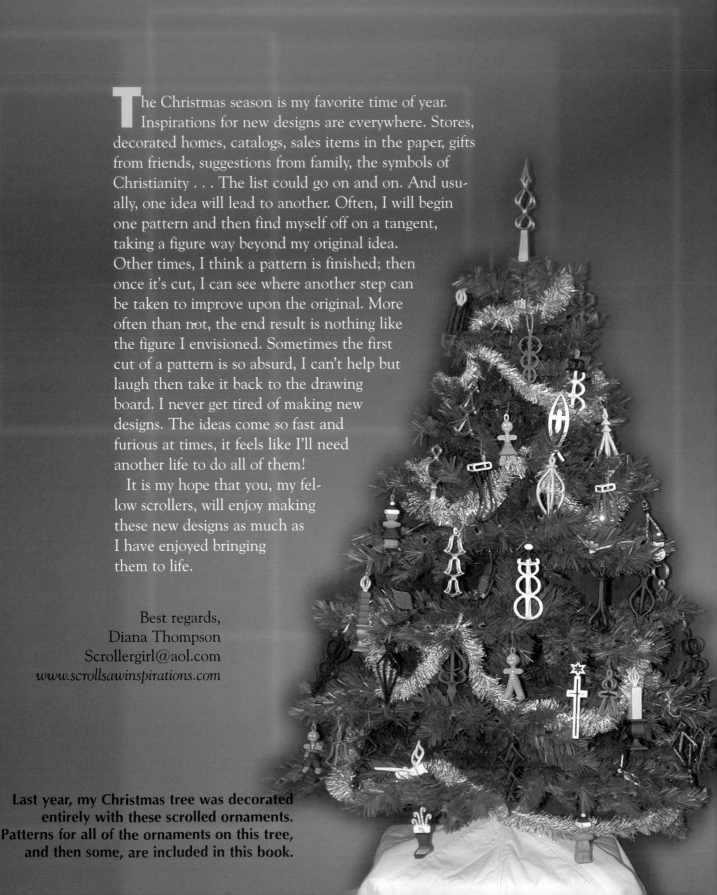

The Christmas season is my favorite time of year. Inspirations for new designs are everywhere. Stores, decorated homes, catalogs, sales items in the paper, gifts from friends, suggestions from family, the symbols of Christianity . . . The list could go on and on. And usually, one idea will lead to another. Often, I will begin one pattern and then find myself off on a tangent, taking a figure way beyond my original idea. Other times, I think a pattern is finished; then once it's cut, I can see where another step can be taken to improve upon the original. More often than not, the end result is nothing like the figure I envisioned. Sometimes the first cut of a pattern is so absurd, I can't help but laugh then take it back to the drawing board. I never get tired of making new designs. The ideas come so fast and furious at times, it feels like I'll need another life to do all of them!

It is my hope that you, my fellow scrollers, will enjoy making these new designs as much as I have enjoyed bringing them to life.

Best regards,
Diana Thompson
Scrollergirl@aol.com
www.scrollsawinspirations.com

Last year, my Christmas tree was decorated entirely with these scrolled ornaments. Patterns for all of the ornaments on this tree, and then some, are included in this book.

Basic Cutting Instructions

Getting Started

Learning to cut compound pieces on your scroll saw is not difficult. It is simply a matter of making your cuts first on one side of the block, then turning the block to make cuts on the adjacent side. There are some basics that you should know, however, before you get started on the patterns in this book.

Safety First

• Make sure all your machinery is working properly. Consult the owner's manual for maintenance and how-to information for each individual tool.

• Wear safety glasses to protect your eyes when you are working around running machinery.

• Do not wear loose clothing that can get caught in machinery.

• Work in a ventilated area and/or wear a mask to protect your lungs from the saw dust.

Cutting Stock

If I am planning to paint the figures, my own personal wood choice for compound projects is sugar pine. Basswood is my second choice; white pine is my third. I find that a close-grained wood works best. Wood with an uneven grain tends to make the blade harder to control and throws it off-line.

Hardwoods are also a good choice for compound figures — if you don't plan to paint the finished piece. You don't want to cover up a beautiful hardwood with paint! The choice of which hardwood to use is wide open. Some woods are quite hard. I try to avoid any wood that is denser than black walnut. Red cedar, cyprus, redwood, willow, magnolia, canary, alder, poplar and Spanish cedar are some of my favorites.

Many of the patterns in this book call for 1½-inch by 1½-inch stock, which is not always easy to find. If you are having trouble finding stock of this thickness, try gluing two pieces of ¾-inch stock together to get the correct thickness.

Tools and Supplies

The lists below outline the basic tools and supplies needed to cut the compound patterns in this book. When special tools are needed, they will be listed within the instructions for that project.

General Tools

- ☐ Scroll saw
- ☐ #5, plain or skip tooth blades
- ☐ Drill or drill press
- ☐ Assorted drill bits
- ☐ Small Quick Grips (optional)
- ☐ Scissors
- ☐ Pony clamps (optional)

General Supplies

- ☐ Spray adhesive
- ☐ ¾" cellophane tape
- ☐ Wood glue
- ☐ 220-grit sandpaper
- ☐ White glue
- ☐ Spare scraps of stock
- ☐ Assorted small brushes
- ☐ Wood sealer
- ☐ Craft paints
- ☐ Clear acrylic spray finish

Finishing Supplies

This information is not meant to be written in stone. I have listed here only the techniques that I use frequently. These techniques are quick and easy, due to my limited time factors.

Experiment on your own and see what marvelous ideas you come up with. If you're new to finishing, I would suggest making a trip to your local craft supply store to check out all the different finishes and paints they have to offer. One scroller by the name of Gail told me she dips figures—the deer in particular—in different colored stains. She uses a darker stain for the antlers and hoofs and a lighter color for the body. One of my greatest joys is to hear what others have done with my patterns!

I seal all the figures I plan to paint with wood sealer, allow them to dry, and then sand them smooth with 220-grit sandpaper. I paint the finished pieces with acrylic craft paints in whatever colors take my fancy. I also mix colors at times to get the special colors I want. When the paints dry, I give the figures a final coat or two of a clear acrylic spray finish.

Danish Oil is an easy stand-by for a natural finish. Just dip the figures in the oil — no brushes, no time consuming methods. The exact directions will be on the product container.

For a super-simple, but still great-looking natural finish, simply seal the figure, allow it to dry, sand it smooth and then apply a clear spray finish. It's just that easy!

Trouble Shooting

For a compound figure to come off the saw uniformly cut, there are a few tips you will need to keep in mind.

Saw Table

An uneven saw table insert can sometimes cause a problem while you are making compound cuts. The figure can fall down into this uneven surface and become distorted. To avoid this, I make a plexiglass top for my saw. I drill a small, ¼-inch hole in the center for inserting the blade. Double-sided tape holds the plexiglass securely to the saw table.

Blades

Tensioning the blade properly is critical to cutting uniform compound figures. A loosely tensioned blade will flex from side to side and cut distorted figures. To tension a blade, keep tightening the tension mechanism until you hear a clear sound when the blade is plucked. If the blade is too loose, the sound will be more of a thud.

Also be sure to check the blade alignment frequently. I have found the best method for checking that the blade is square to the table is to make a shallow cut into a piece of scrap wood. Then I turn the wood around to the back of the blade (do not turn it upside down) and slide the back of the moving blade back into the cut. If it slides in nicely, the table is square. (You'll find more tidbits like this in John Nelson's book *Scroll Saw Workbook*.)

Another thing to keep in mind is that blades need to be changed often. Trying to get too much "mileage" out of a blade will result in you pushing too hard against the blade, which will distort the blade and the figures.

Finally, make sure you are not pushing the blade sideways as you cut. Every now and then, ease up on the work, allow the blade to right itself, then continue sawing.

Helpful Tips

I recommend sawing to the waste side of the pattern lines for the best results. Sawing right on the lines will result in removing too much material, which will cause some of the more delicate patterns, such as the deer antlers, to break easily.

When using harder, denser wood, cover the stock with clear packing tape first, then apply the pattern. The work will go much faster and easier. Applying the tape before the pattern avoids glare off the shiny tape from the shop lights.

Don't be afraid to use plenty of spray adhesive. The patterns won't need to be removed as is the case with fretwork. Extra adhesive will also allow you to slide the pattern around to the proper position.

If the pattern you are working on has legs, such as the deer, cut the space between the legs first. If your pattern has frets (inside cuts), such as the ornaments, make the inside cuts first. Cut the frets on both sides and leave all the frets in place as you make the outside cuts. This gives your piece some extra stability as you scroll.

General Directions

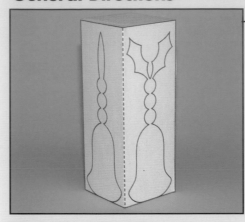

Step 1. Cut the pattern out around the rectangular line. Fold the pattern in half along the dashed line. Apply spray adhesive to the back of the pattern. Adhere the pattern around two sides of the stock using the dashed line as a guide.

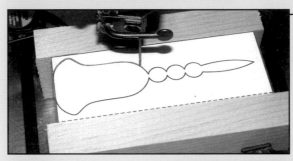

Step 2. Cut the left side in one continuous line. Stay to the waste side of the pattern lines.

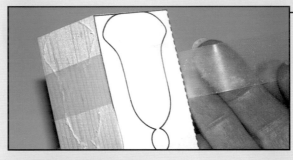

Step 3. Allowing the figure to rest naturally in the block, pinch the block and the figure together and apply tape around the block with ¾-inch cellophane tape. The taller figures will need to be taped in two places.

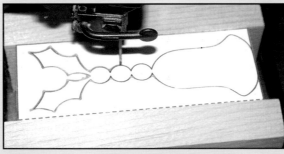

Step 4. Cut the right side in one continuous line. Stay to the waste side of the pattern lines. Tip: Don't push on the bottom of the block while cutting. This will cause the figures to become distorted.

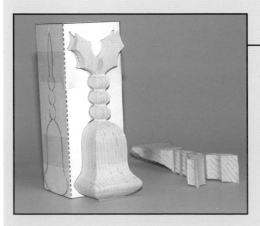

Step 5. Gently remove the figure from the block. Note: With the more delicate figures, such as the deer, hold the block firmly between your fingers and slide the figure out the back side of the block.

Icicle Ornaments

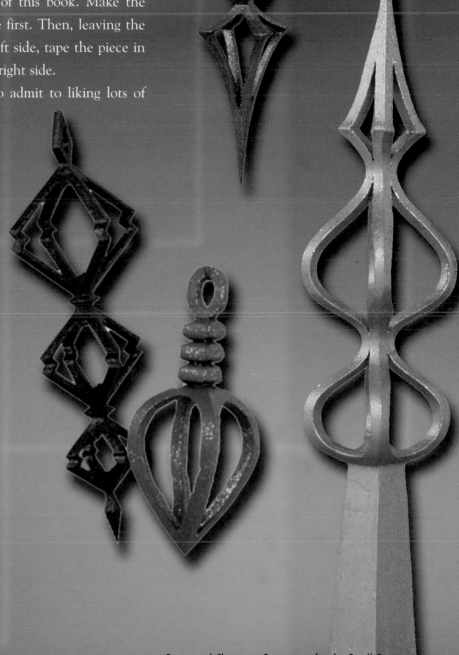

Last year, our tree was decorated entirely with these scrolled ornaments. I even created an ornament for my favorite puppy dog, Bailey, my daughter's beloved goldie. (See page 26.)

All the patterns are cut using the general directions at the beginning of this book. Make the inside cuts on each side first. Then, leaving the frets in place, cut the left side, tape the piece in two places, and cut the right side.

At this point, I have to admit to liking lots of sparkle and glitter. I painted many of the ornaments with metallic paints and then top coated each with glitter paint. When using the glitter paint there is no need to apply a clear spray finish; the paint dries clear and shiny.

Teardrop

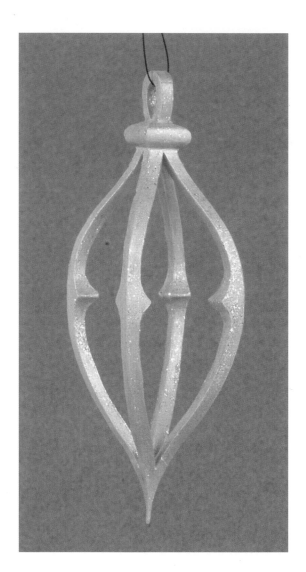

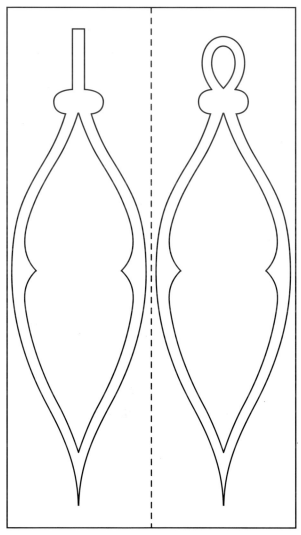

© Diana Thompson

Transformation

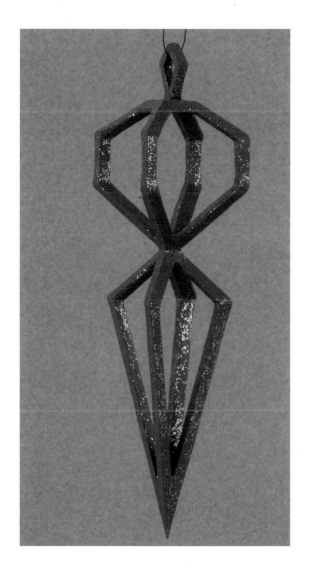

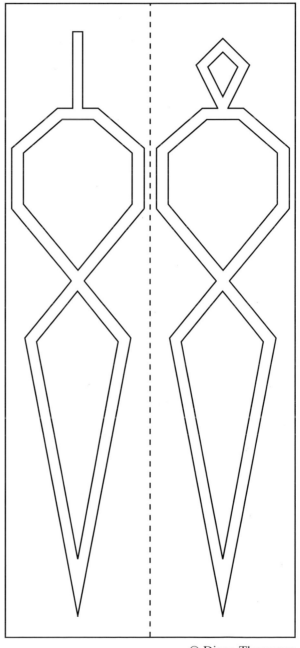

© Diana Thompson

Melting Sphere

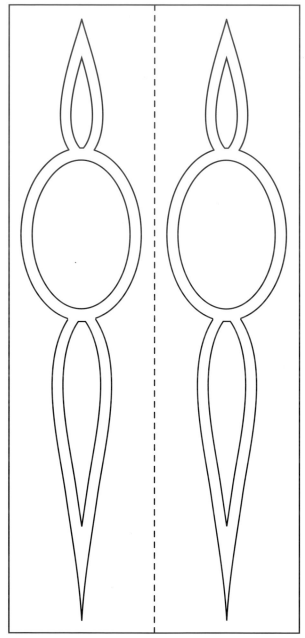

© Diana Thompson

Dangling Diamonds

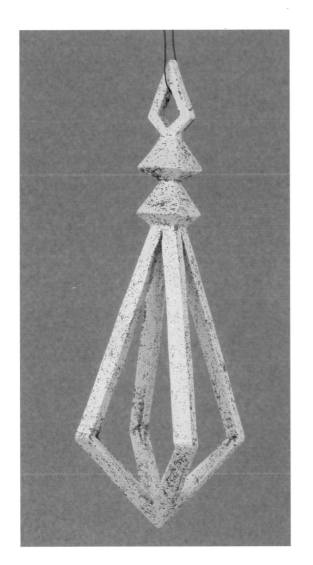

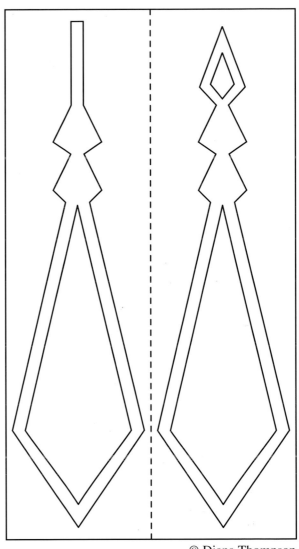

© Diana Thompson

Droplet

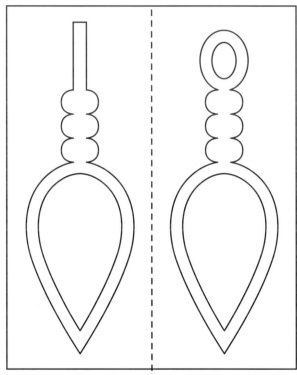

© Diana Thompson

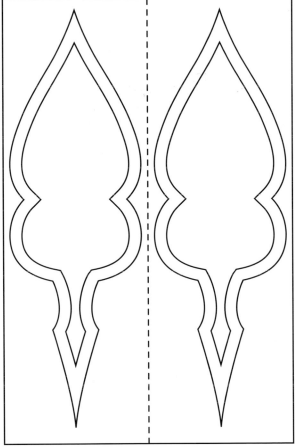

© Diana Thompson

Triple Spheres

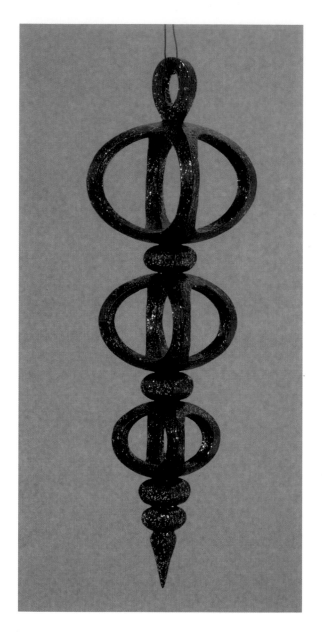

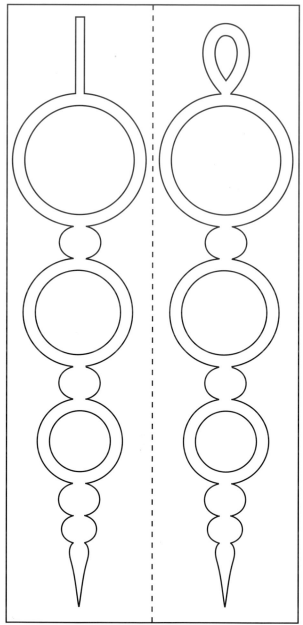

© Diana Thompson

Spire

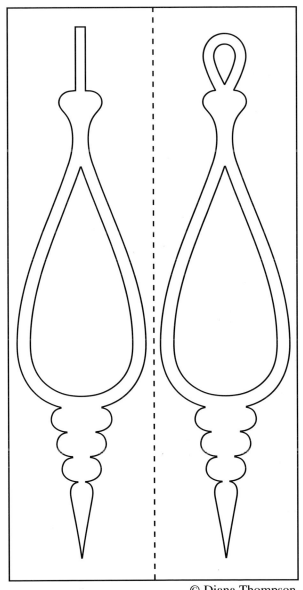

© Diana Thompson

Icicle

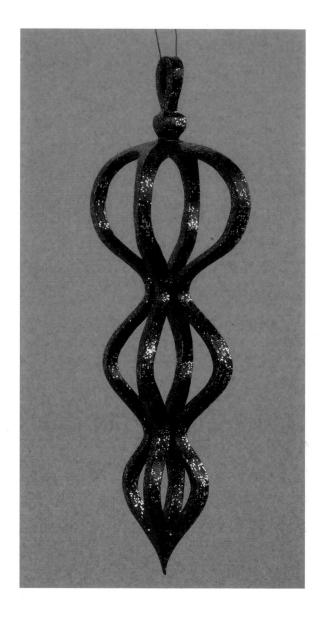

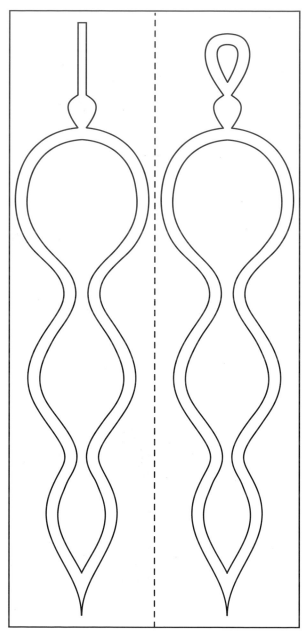

© Diana Thompson

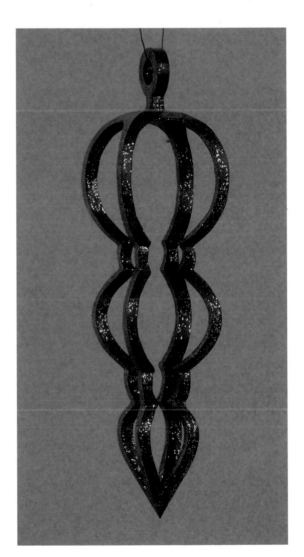

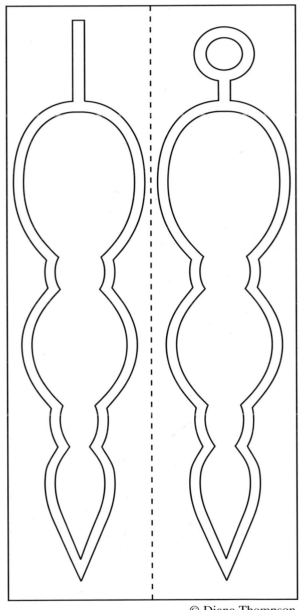

© Diana Thompson

Triplet

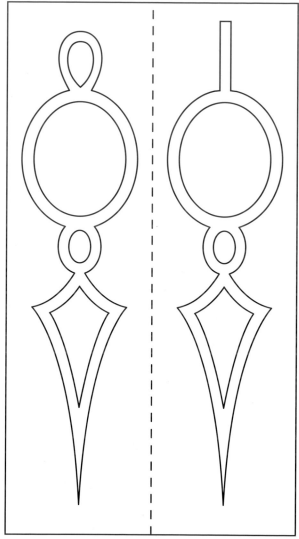

© Diana Thompson

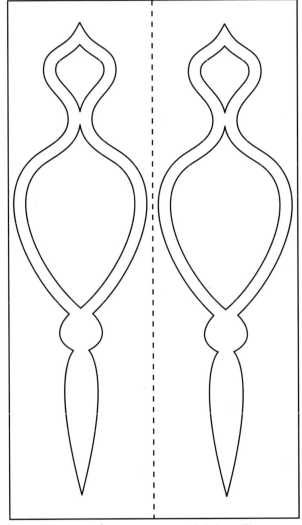

© Diana Thompson

Triple Diamonds

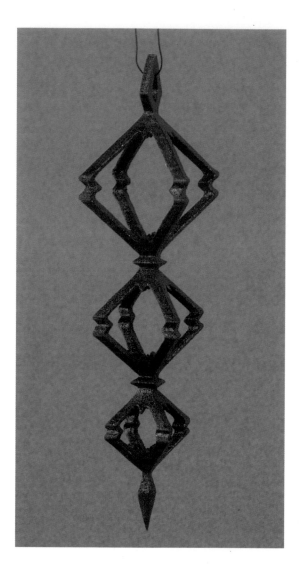

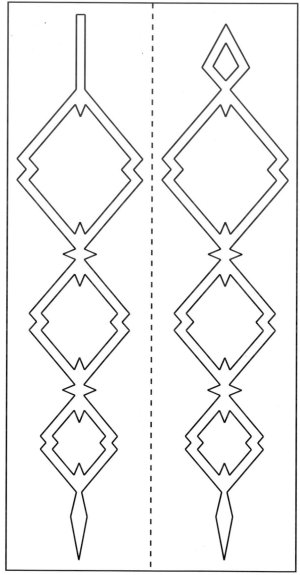

© Diana Thompson

Descent

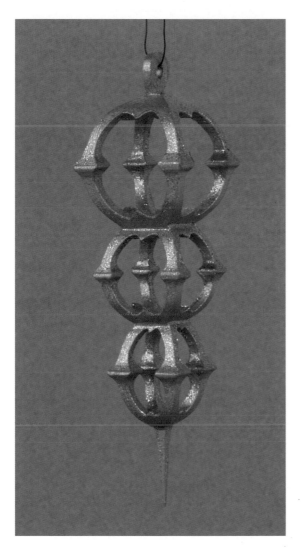

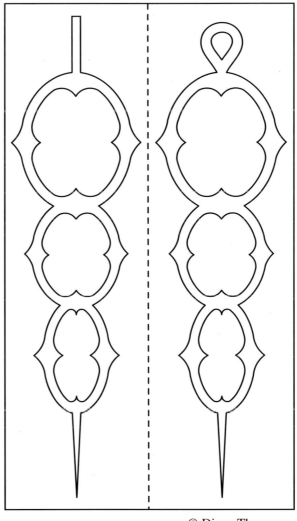

© Diana Thompson

Gravity

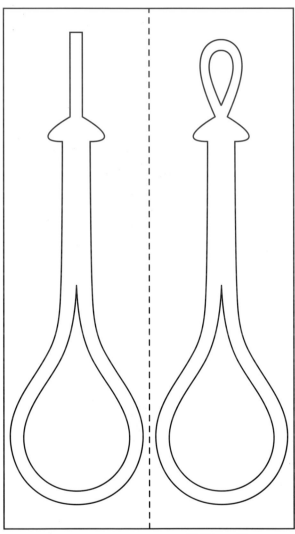

© Diana Thompson

3-D Diamond

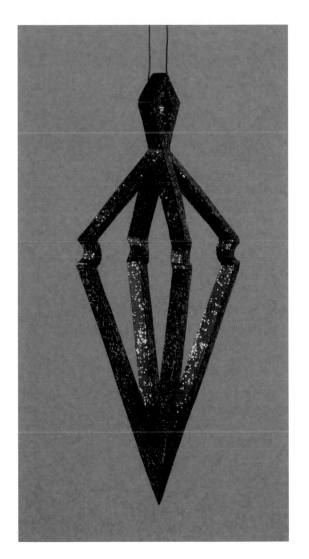

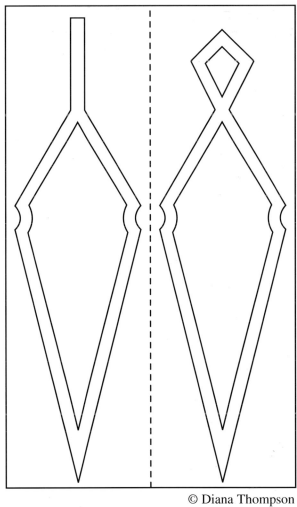

© Diana Thompson

Steps

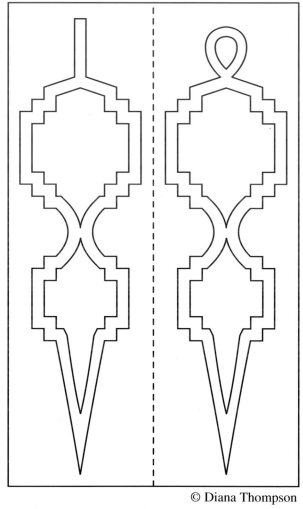

© Diana Thompson

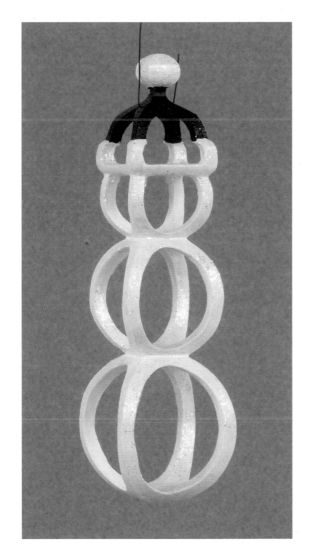

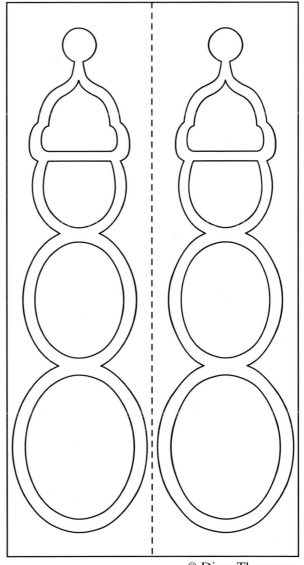

© Diana Thompson

Blazing Cross

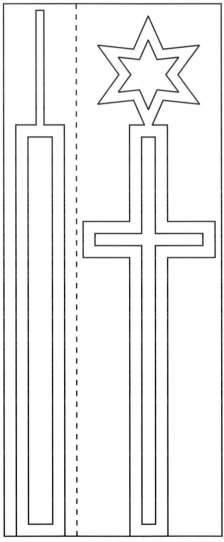

© Diana Thompson

Christmas Tree

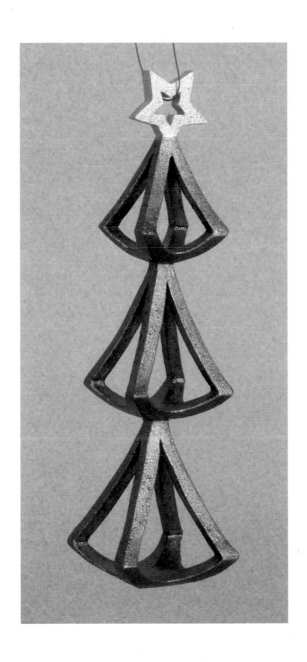

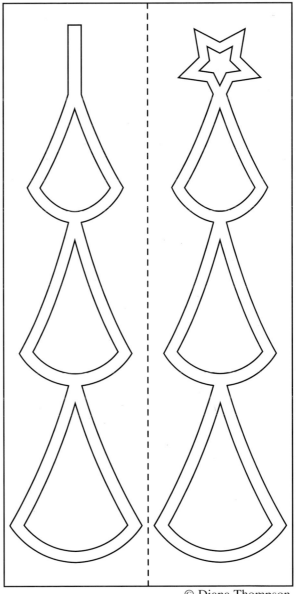

© Diana Thompson

Christmas Stocking

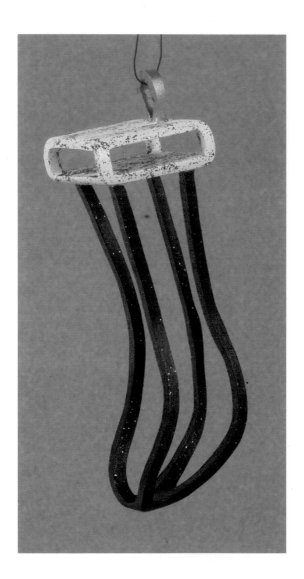

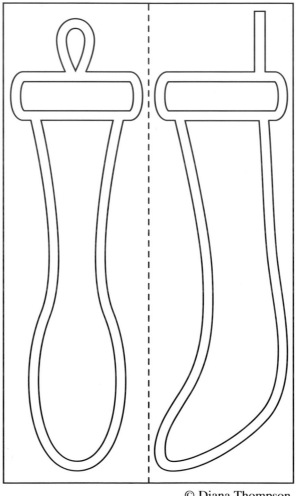

© Diana Thompson

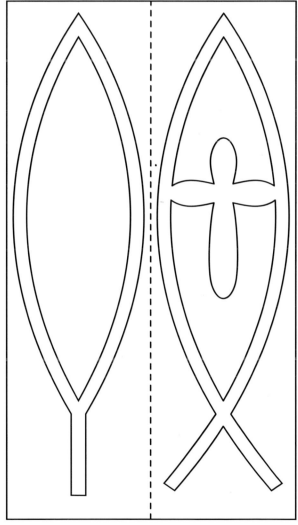

© Diana Thompson

Special Treat

Mitten

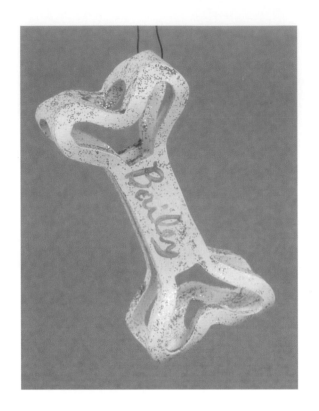

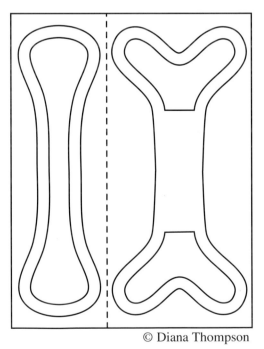

© Diana Thompson

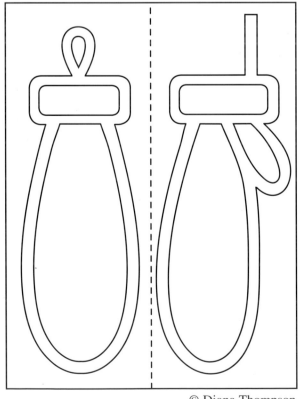

© Diana Thompson

Gingerbread Man

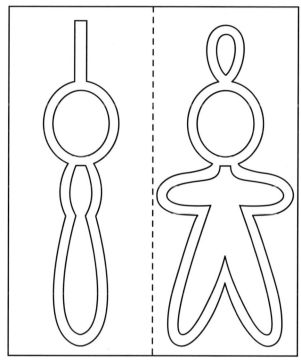

© Diana Thompson

Flaming Candle

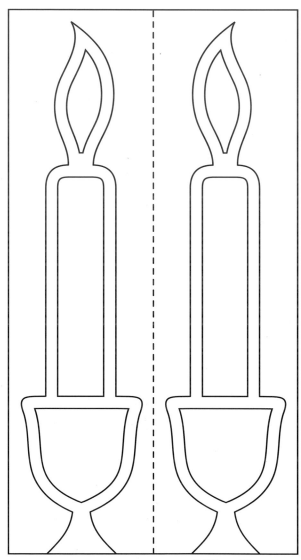

© Diana Thompson

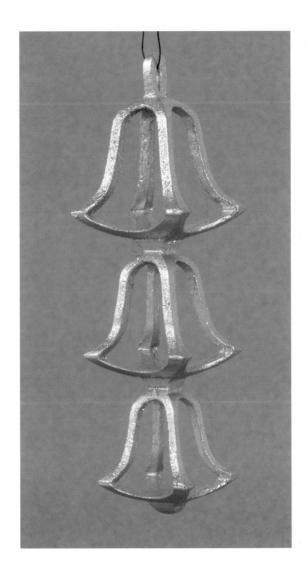

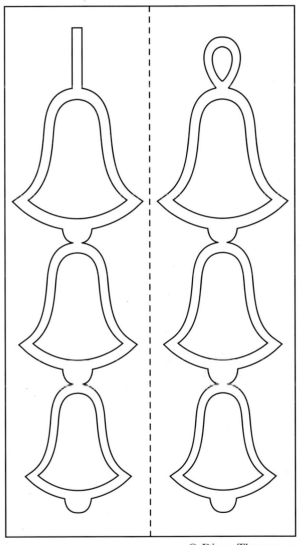

© Diana Thompson

Tree Topper

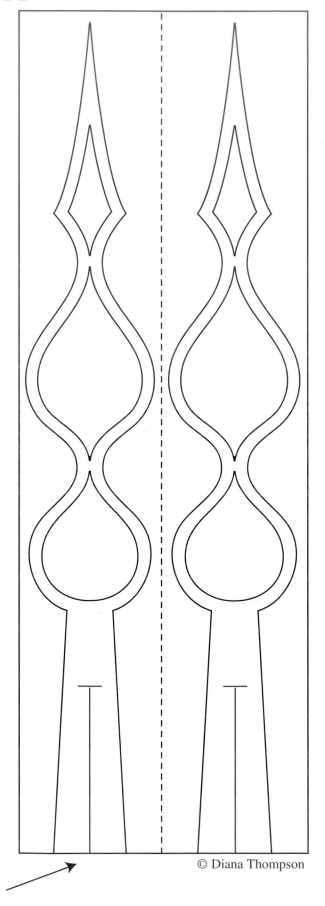

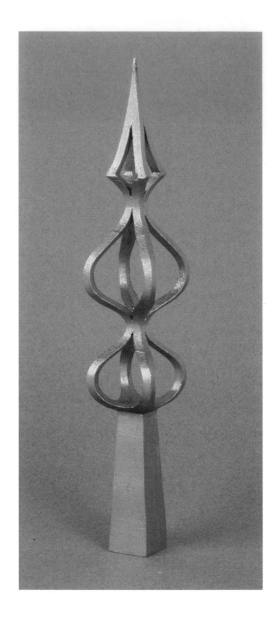

© Diana Thompson

Depth lines

Drill a hole in the bottom to the depth line with a 3/8" Forstner bit. Cut out as usual.

Traditional Ornaments

Most of these figures can hang on your tree or just sit around as decorations during the holiday season. Traditional ornaments also provide a great opportunity to experiment with different finishes. I finished the teddy bears on page 35 with flocking, which gives a felt-like appearance and texture. To the Christmas trees on pages 40 and 41 I added a touch of decorative snow for a festive look. Both of these finishing materials—and many more— are available at your local craft store. Have fun; try everything!

Gingerbread Boy

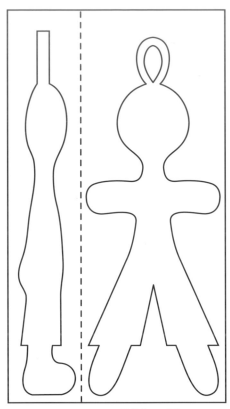

© Diana Thompson

Gingerbread Girl

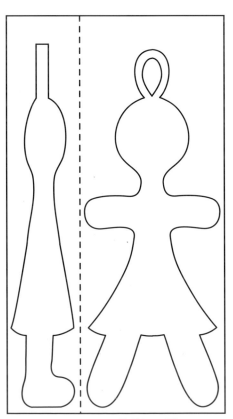

Remove the hanger at the top to create a table-top gingerbread family.

© Diana Thompson

Gingerbread Man

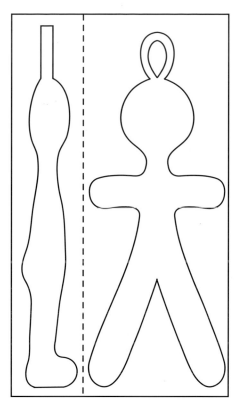

Four Candy Canes

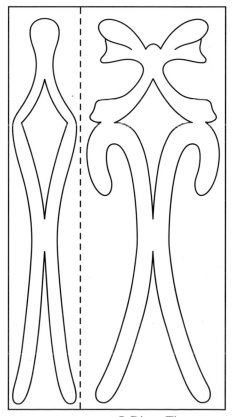

Holly Bell

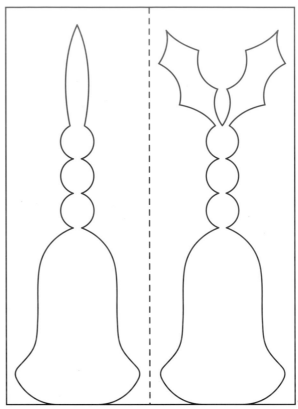

© Diana Thompson

Sweet Stocking

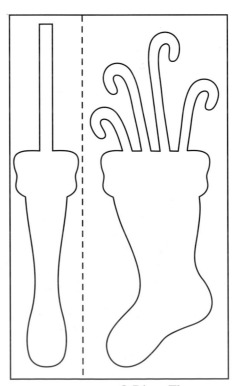

© Diana Thompson

Teddy Bear Girl

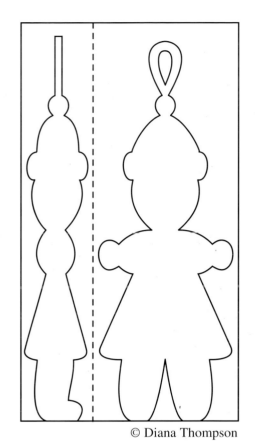

© Diana Thompson

Teddy Bear Boy

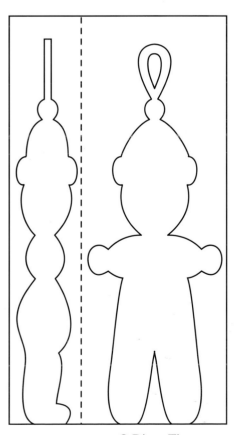

© Diana Thompson

**Remove the hanger at the top to create a
table-top teddy bear family**

Mrs. Claus

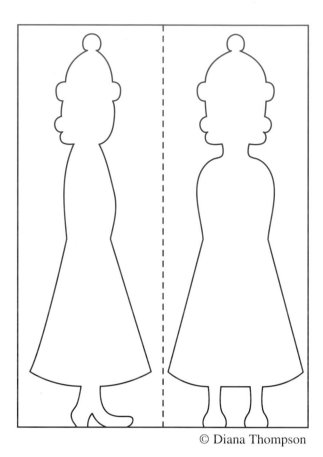

© Diana Thompson

Fold this section over top of stock

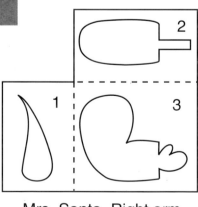

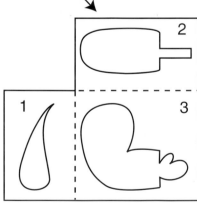

Mrs. Santa Right arm
Cut 1

Mrs. Santa   Left arm
Cut 1

Make arms cuts according to
numbered sequence.

Glue arms to body.

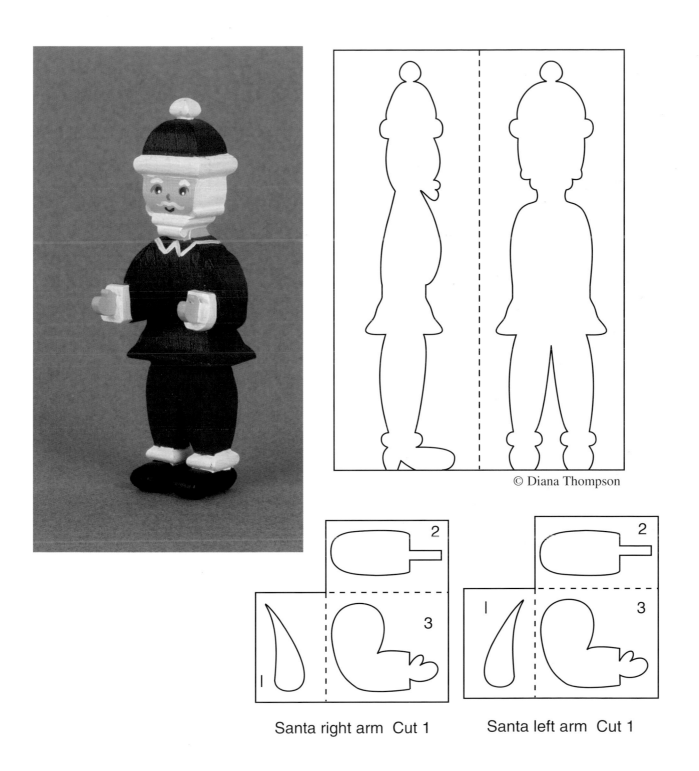

© Diana Thompson

Santa right arm Cut 1   Santa left arm Cut 1

Ice Skating Snowman

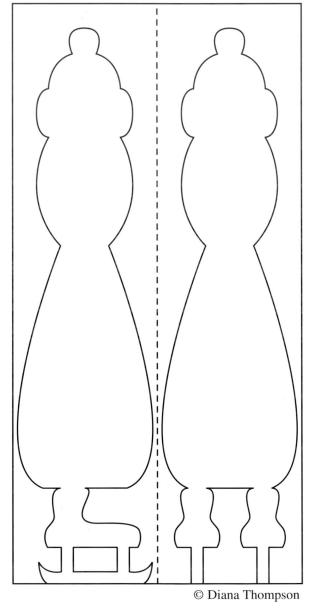

© Diana Thompson

Silly Snowman

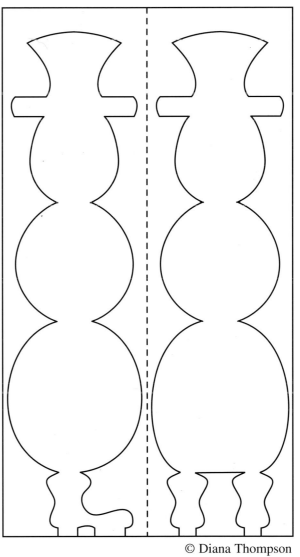

© Diana Thompson

Snowy Tree

© Diana Thompson

Chubby Snowman

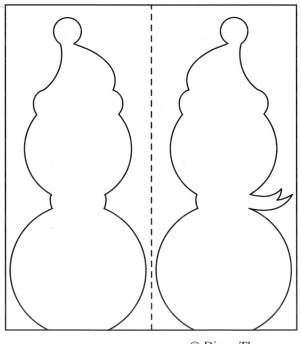

© Diana Thompson

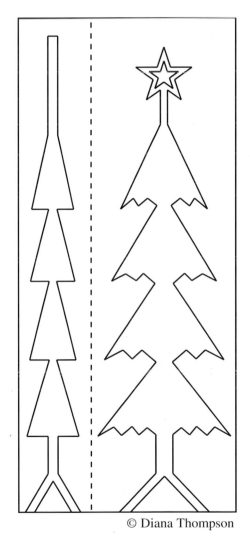

© Diana Thompson

Burning Bright

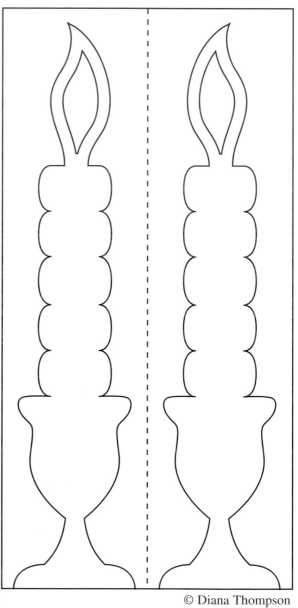

© Diana Thompson

Evening Glow

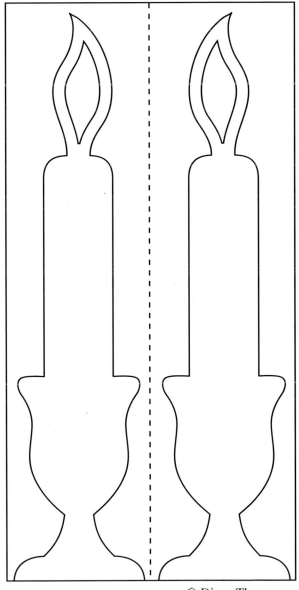

© Diana Thompson

Chilly Penguin

Wing placement →

© Diana Thompson

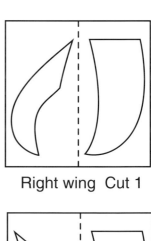

Right wing Cut 1

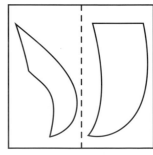

Left wing Cut 1

Winged Ornaments

The angels in this section were the first two-part patterns I attempted. After the angels turned out so well, I got carried away and put wings on everything ! The swan is an adaptation of the original swan pattern in my first book.

After cutting out the patterns, simply glue the wings into the notch on the body and finish the pieces as desired. Metallic paints and sparkle coats make great finishes for these flying ornaments.

Dove of Peace

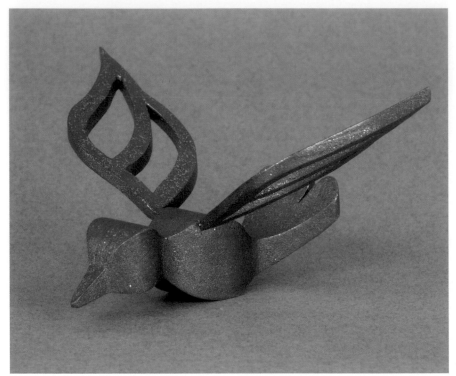

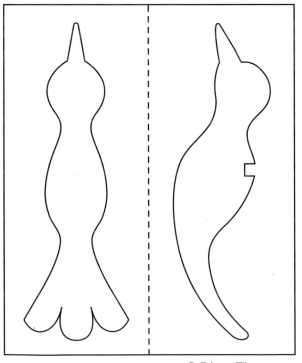

© Diana Thompson

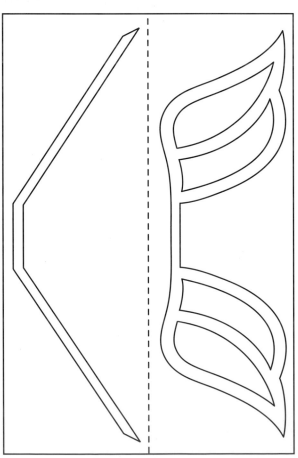

Guardian Angel

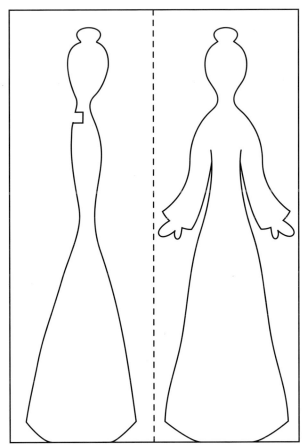

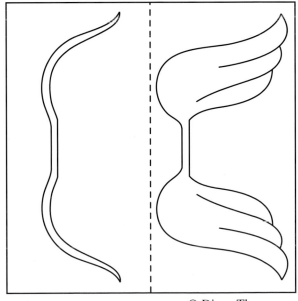

© Diana Thompson

Angel of Light

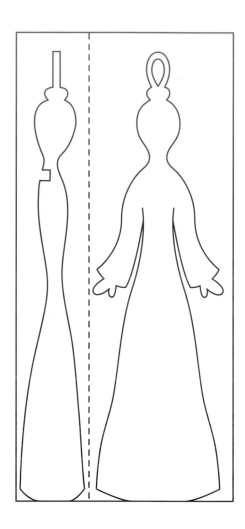

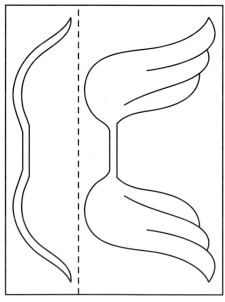

© Diana Thompson

Heralding Angel

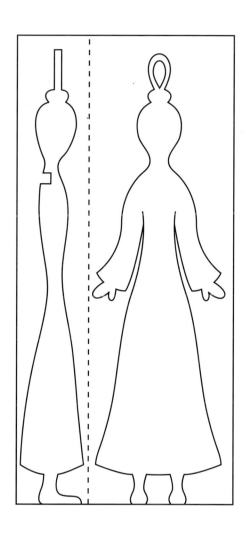

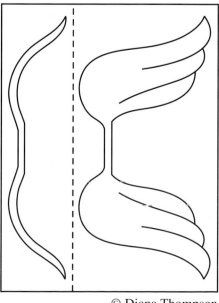

Christmas Swan

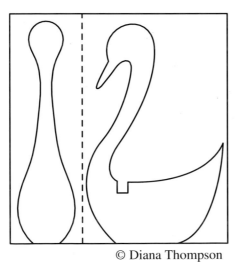
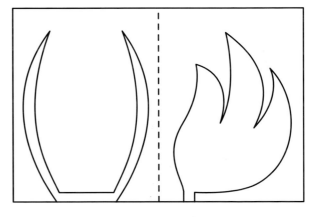

© Diana Thompson

Compound Projects

What would the holiday season be without all the decorations that come out of storage to brighten up our homes during this festive season?

All of the projects on the following pages are designed to adorn table tops, shelves, mantels… You name it; these projects will be perfect.

Follow the basic cutting instructions at the beginning of this book to cut the projects. Assembly directions and special weighting options are discussed on the pattern pages for each individual project. Again, experiment and have fun with finish.

Napkin Rings

Dress up your table during the holiday season with these festive napkin rings. These were inspired by a kind gentleman I met in Pennsylvania during the Fox Chapel Open House 2001.

Cut all the patterns according to general directions at the beginning of this book and finish as desired. I used acrylic craft paints with metallic accents for the samples pictured in this section.

Mr. Kringle

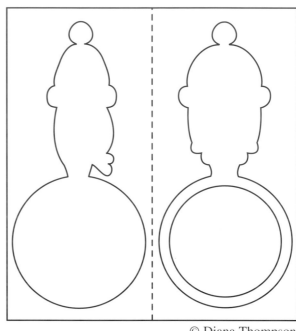

© Diana Thompson

Mrs. Kringle

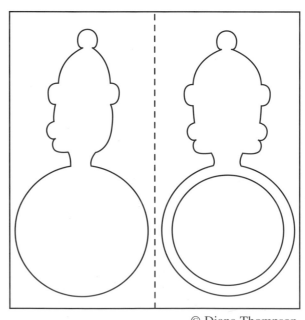

© Diana Thompson

Festive Branches

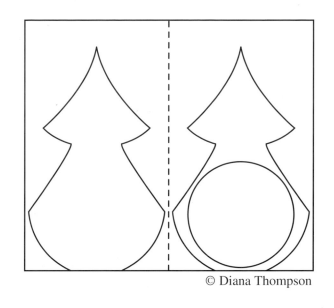

© Diana Thompson

Friendly Snowman

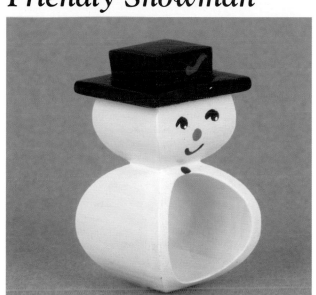

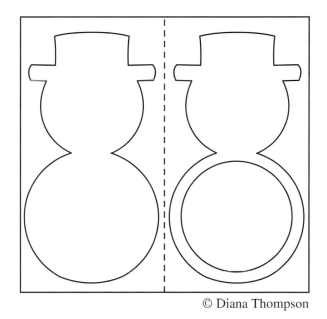

© Diana Thompson

Gold Tones

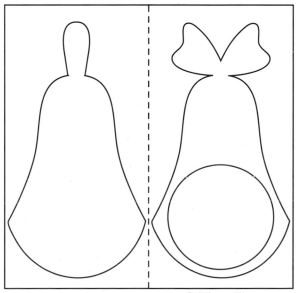

© Diana Thompson

Snowmen Candlesticks

This is what happens when a designer becomes fascinated with Forstner bits: She drills holes in everything! These compound candlesticks are the perfect example. I altered a snowman pattern to fit a hole big enough for standard taper candles, then drilled a hole in the top for the candles and in the bottom for a counterweight. It's a simple technique. Try it on some of your other favorite holiday patterns.

Special Tools

⅞" Forstner bit for top opening
½" Forstner bit for bottom opening

Special Supplies
1 oz. egg sinker (This is simply an egg-shaped lead fishing weight, found at a local superstore)
1 – 6 X 1¼" flathead screw or epoxy glue

Directions

1. After applying the pattern to the wood, measure and mark the center point on the top and the bottom.
2. Using the ⅞" Forstner bit, drill to the depth line on the top.
3. Using the ½" Forstner bit, repeat the process on the bottom.
4. Cut the piece out according to the general directions at the beginning of this book.
5. Glue the weight into the bottom hole with epoxy. You may also choose to secure the weight with a screw, in which case the opening in the weight will need to be enlarged with a ⁹⁄₆₄" bit.
6. To give the figure a more realistic appearance, mix a little texture building compound to the white paint. Finish the details as desired and top coat the entire piece with a clear glitter paint. I got carried away and glittered the candles, too!

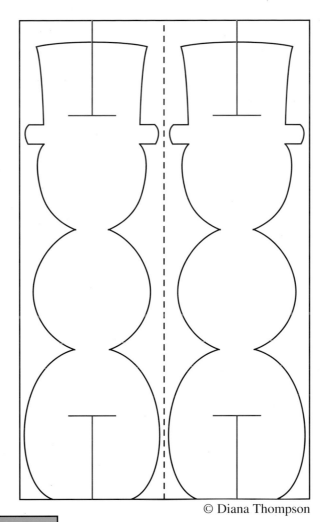

© Diana Thompson

Mark the center point on the top and bottom of the stock.

Using the center point as a guide, drill a hole to accept the weight.

Projects

Poinsettia Vase

This lovely vase of bright poinsettias was a challenge to design. Fortunately, it's easier to cut than it was to develop. Some assembly is required.

Special Tools

⅞" Forstner bit
Weight bashing jig (directions below)

Special Supplies

1 oz. egg sinker (This is simply an egg-shaped fishing weight, found at your local superstore.)
1 – 4 X ⅞" flathead screw or epoxy glue

Making the weight jig

To make the weight jig, use the ⅞" Forstner bit to drill a hole in a ¼-inch-thick piece of spare stock. Place the egg sinker inside and bash it down with a hammer until the weight is even with the top of the jig.

The weight can be secured in the bottom hole with epoxy glue. You may also choose to attach the weight with a flathead screw, in which case the center hole will need to be enlarged with a ³⁄₃₂" drill bit.

Directions

1. Mark and drill the top and bottom holes in the vase with a ⅞" Forstner bit.
2. Cut the vase out according to the general directions in the front of this book.
3. Cut out all of the poinsettia pieces according to the general directions. Each flower needs one stem, eight "petals," and four leaves.
4. Glue the first set of petals (petals 1). There will be a small gap between the petals and the stamen.
5. Glue the leaves into place below the first set of petals.
6. Apply the glue and tuck the tips of the second set of petals into the gaps between the first set of petals and the stamen.

Depth lines

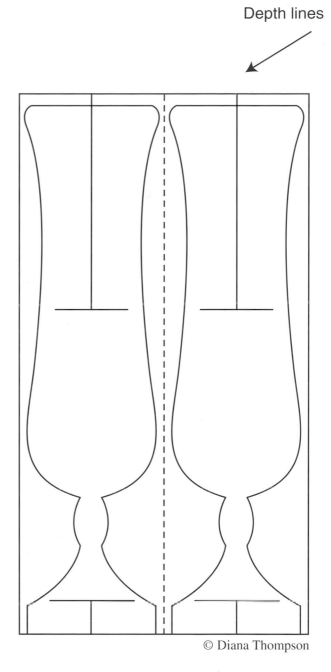

© Diana Thompson

Make a "weight bashing jig" by drilling a hole into a ¼-inch piece of spare stock.

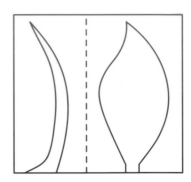

Petal 1   Cut 4 for each poinsettia

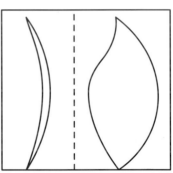

Petal 2   Cut 4 for each poinsettia

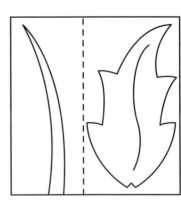

Leaf   Cut 4 for each poinsettia

© Diana Thompson

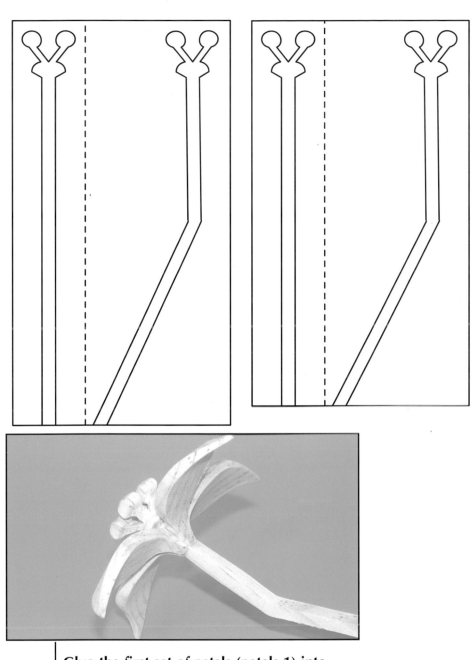

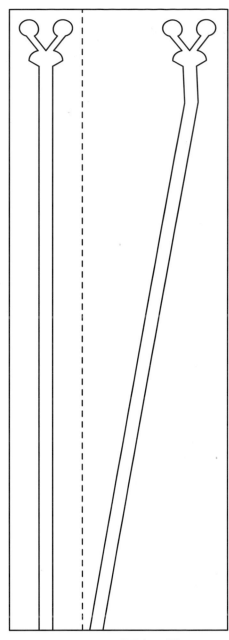

© Diana Thompson

Glue the first set of petals (petals 1) into place on the stem.

Glue the leaves into place below the first set of petals.

Glue the second set of petals into place just below the stamen.

Sleigh and Reindeer

I've added some small holiday decorations and ribbon to make this simple sleigh into a dashing display for a table or mantle. Tip: To hold the reins in place inside the sleigh, simply tie the ribbon ends through a bolt and drop the bolt in the front of the sleigh.

Cut all of the figures according to the general directions in the front of this book. The dashed lines on the sleigh pattern show how to assemble the project. Finish as desired.

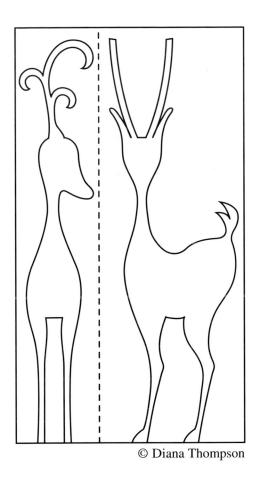

© Diana Thompson

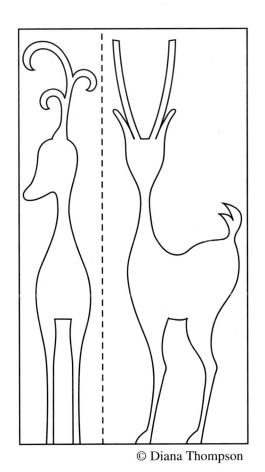

© Diana Thompson

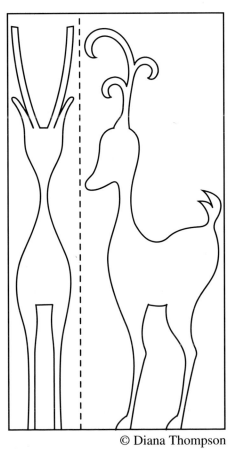

© Diana Thompson

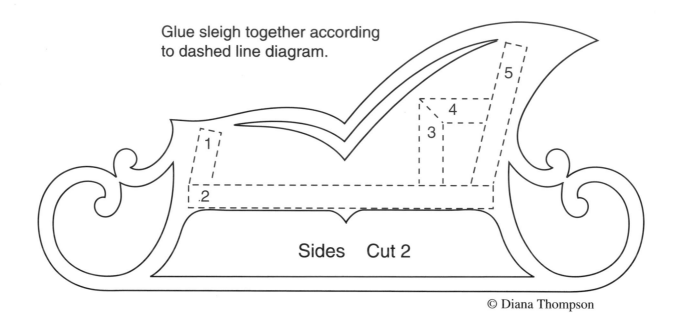

Glue sleigh together according to dashed line diagram.

Sides   Cut 2

© Diana Thompson

1 Toe
   Cut 1

   20 degree angle

3 45 degree angle

   Seat front cut 1

2

Floor
Cut 1

4 15 degree angle

   Seat, cut 1

   45 degree angle

5

Back
Cut one

15 degree angle

Nativity Scene

This simple, yet elegant nativity scene will hold a cherished spot in your home year after year. I added only three animals —a sheep, a donkey and a cow—but you could easily add others.

All of the figures, except the arms, are cut using the general directions in the beginning of this book. The arms have three cuts and should be cut in the sequence indicated on the patterns. I have found it easier to seal and sand each piece before assembling the individual figures. Note: I used pieces of raffia for the hay in the manger. The raffia is glued in place, then the baby Jesus is glued on top. I also used raffia for the burro's lead.

Finish all of the figures according to the photo or as desired. I find it easier to use a clear spray finish on the individual figures before gluing them to the base. Paint the base and star burst as desired. Glue the star burst in place, then use a clear spray finish. Glue all figures onto the base and you're done.

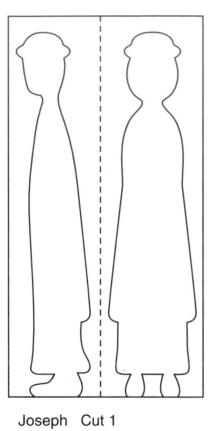

Joseph   Cut 1

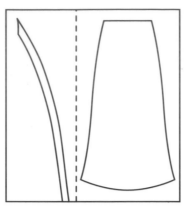

Joseph Headdress Cut 1

This section is folded
over the top of the stock.

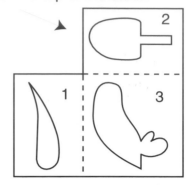

Joseph Right arm   Cut 1

Make arms cuts according to
numbered sequence.

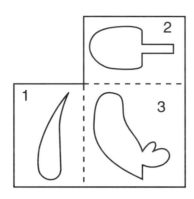

Joseph Left arm   Cut 1

© Diana Thompson

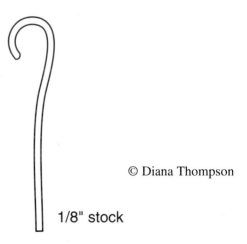

1/8" stock

Staff   Cut 1

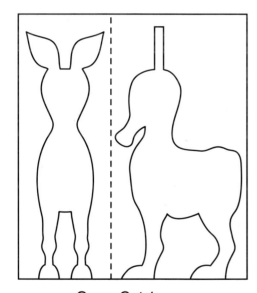

Cow   Cut 1

Lamb   Cut 1

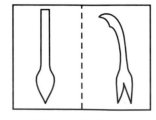

Cow tail Cut 1

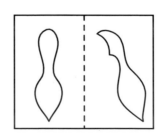

Burro tail   Cut 1

Burro   Cut 1

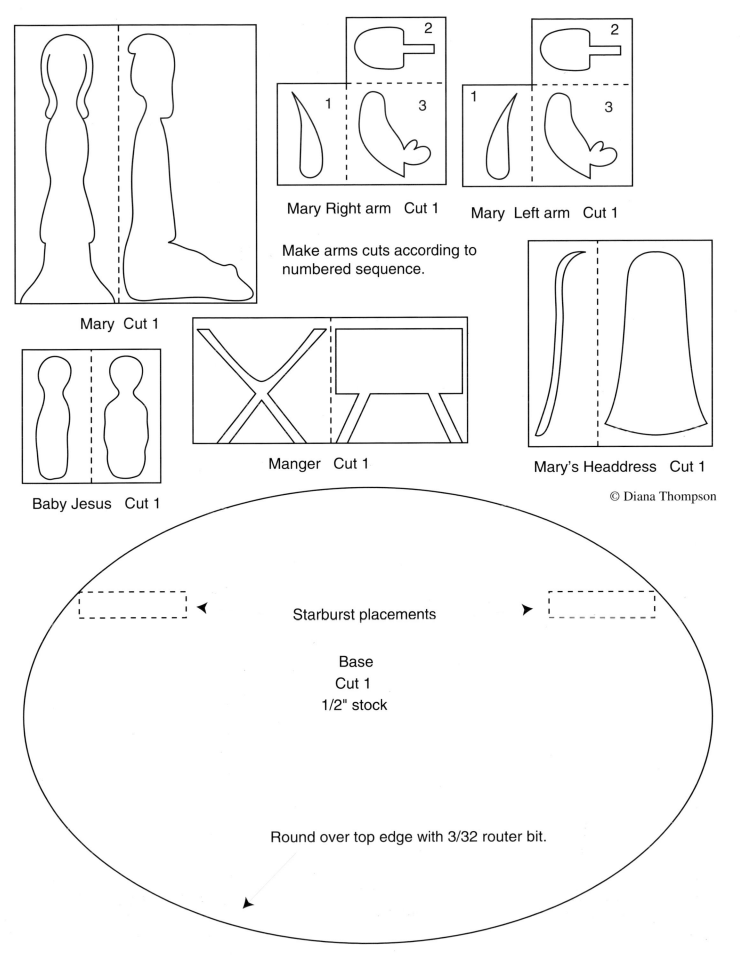

Mary Right arm   Cut 1

Mary Left arm   Cut 1

Make arms cuts according to numbered sequence.

Mary   Cut 1

Baby Jesus   Cut 1

Manger   Cut 1

Mary's Headdress   Cut 1

© Diana Thompson

Starburst placements

Base
Cut 1
1/2" stock

Round over top edge with 3/32 router bit.

Starburst
Cut 1
1/4" stock

Glue starburst to base.

© Diana Thompson

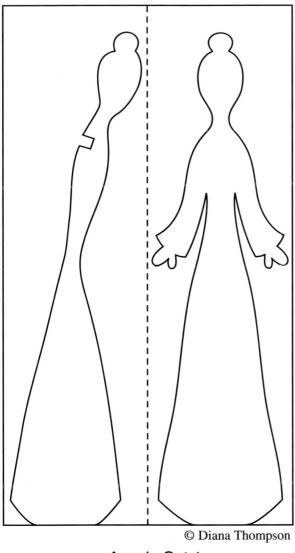

© Diana Thompson

Angel   Cut 1

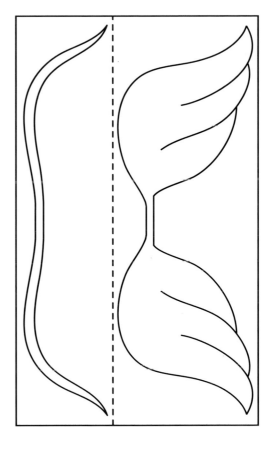

Wings   Cut 1

Glue wings into notch of angel body.